SPACE VEHICLES

by Anne Rockwell and David Brion

Dutton Children's Books · New York

For Julianna Joy

A.R. and D.B.

The author and illustrator would like to thank NASA and the Johnson Space Center for providing reference material.

Copyright © 1994 by Anne Rockwell and David Brion
All rights reserved.

CIP Data is available.

Published in the United States 1994 by
Dutton Children's Books,
a division of Penguin Books USA Inc.
375 Hudson Street, New York, New York 10014
Printed in Hong Kong
First Edition
1 3 5 7 9 10 8 6 4 2
ISBN 0-525-45270-2

Rockets blast off!

They carry space vehicles
up into the blue sky,

far away from our planet,
Earth, out into black space.

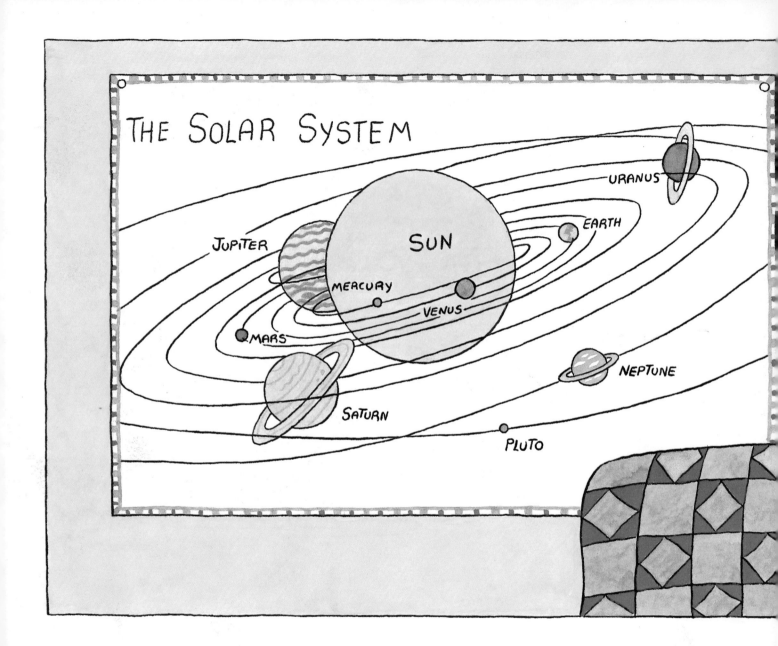

Space is where our sun and moon,
the stars, and other planets are.

To travel so far,
space vehicles go very fast.

Satellites are space vehicles that go into orbit around Earth. Some tell us what the weather will be.

Probes go to other planets
and send pictures back to Earth.

Lunar modules look like giant insects.
They take astronauts to the moon that I see at night.

Lunar rovers look like cars.
They have wide wheels to ride through moon dust.

Space shuttles take off with rockets,

but land like planes.

Astronauts float weightless

inside the space shuttle.

Astronauts use space vehicles called *flying armchairs*

to go outside the shuttle and fix broken satellites.

A ground crew stays behind on Earth

to help space vehicles find their way.

One day there will be big laboratories on space stations that stay in space for a long time.

Scientists will use space vehicles to go there.
They will study and learn, then come home to Earth.

I will be a scientist one day.

I will use space vehicles to learn about

beautiful, mysterious outer space.